SHARKS, SHARKS, SHARKS

First Steck-Vaughn Edition 1992

Copyright © 1989 American Teacher Publications

Published by Steck-Vaughn Company

Library of Congress number: 89-3666

Library of Congress Cataloging in Publication Data.

Anton, Tina.
 Sharks, sharks, sharks / Tina Anton; illustrated by Grace Goldberg.

 (Real readers)
 Summary: Discusses the physical characteristics, behavior, and habitat of sharks.
 1. Sharks—Juvenile literature. [1. Sharks.] I. Goldberg, Grace, ill. II. Title. III. Series.
QL638.9.A58   1989   597′.31—dc19   89-3666

ISBN 0-8172-3531-0   hardcover library binding

ISBN 0-8114-6731-7   softcover binding

      6 7 8 9 0   96 95

SHARKS SHARKS SHARKS

by Tina Anton

illustrated by Grace Goldberg

RSVP

RAINTREE
STECK-VAUGHN
PUBLISHERS
The Steck-Vaughn Company

Austin, Texas

SPLASH! Dr. Eugenie Clark dives down into the sea.

Eugenie Clark is a scientist who likes to study sharks. Other scientists like to study sharks, too. Sometimes they study sharks in the sea. And sometimes they take sharks and bring them to a lab.

Some of the things that they have learned may surprise you.

nurse shark

A shark cannot live if it is not in water.
Most sharks live in the sea. But sometimes
a shark will swim from the sea into a
river. One kind of shark lives in a lake.
No one knows how the sharks got there.

bull shark

There are many kinds of sharks. Scientists have named more than 350 kinds. Some sharks are little. The dwarf shark is very little. It can fit in your hand.

Some sharks are big. The whale shark is as big as a bus. It is the biggest shark of all.

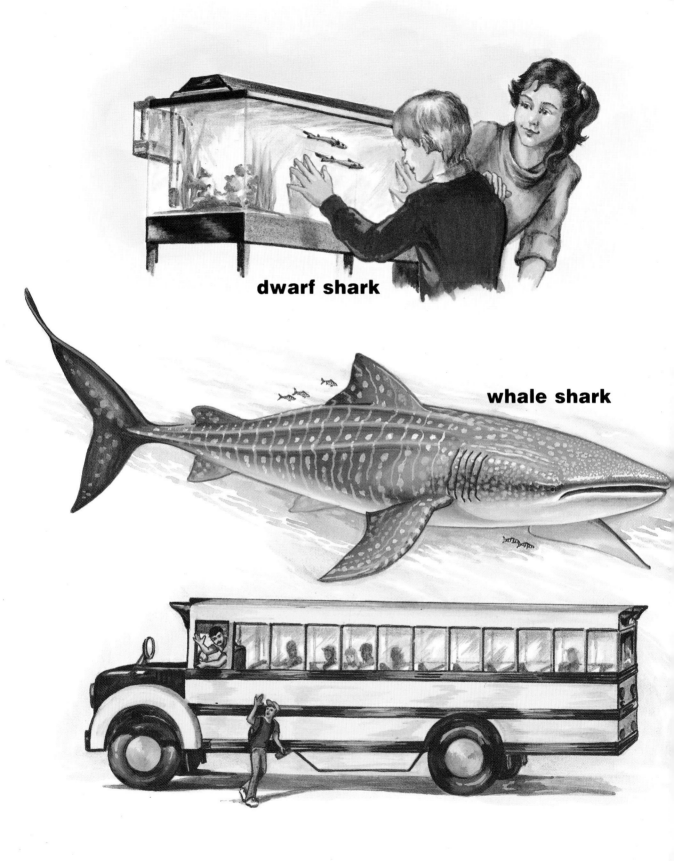

dwarf shark

whale shark

All sharks have a big fin on their backs. But not all sharks look the same. The tiger shark has stripes. The leopard shark has spots. The hammerhead shark has a head shaped like a hammer. The angel shark has fins that look like wings.

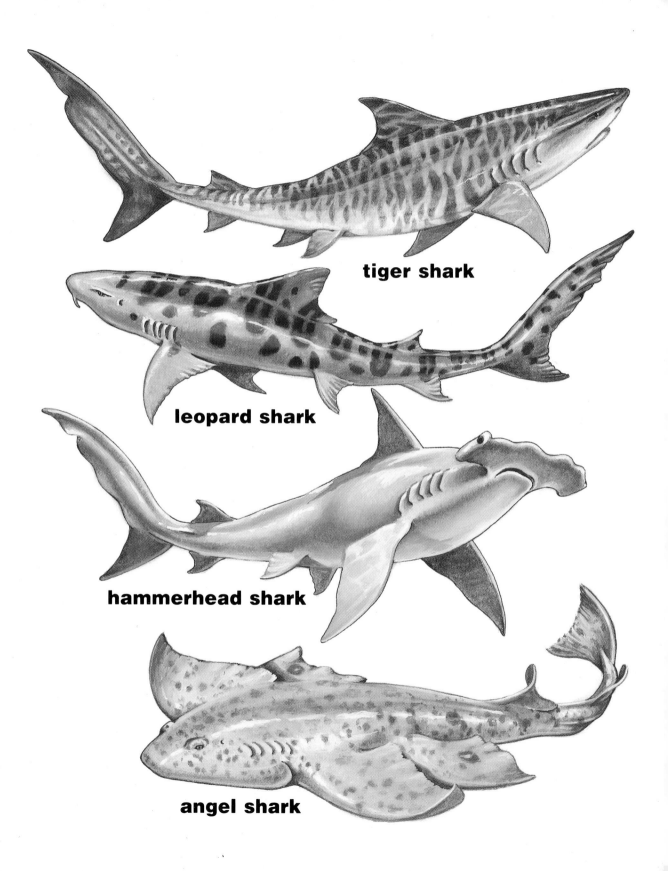

tiger shark

leopard shark

hammerhead shark

angel shark

If you could rub a shark's skin you might get a cut! Its skin feels like sandpaper! That is because a shark's skin is made up of very small, hard teeth. These very small teeth are called denticles.

shark skin

Most fish have something inside of them
called a swim bladder. The swim bladder
is like a balloon. It helps them to float.
But a shark does not have a swim bladder
inside of it. It cannot float. A shark must
swim, or it will sink.

great white shark

Sharks are very good hunters. They use their noses to help them find food. A shark can smell food far away in the sea.

Sharks use hearing to help them hunt, too. Sharks hear very well, but they do not have ears.

A shark uses its skin to hear. A shark "feels" a noise in the water with its skin. A shark's skin "feels" a thing move in the water. A shark's skin tells the shark where a fish is. Then the shark can swim to the fish.

At the end of its hunt, a shark uses its eyes. Scientists used to think that sharks could not see well. But sharks can see things that are close by.

When a shark gets close to food, the shark sees it. Then the shark grabs or bites the food and eats it!

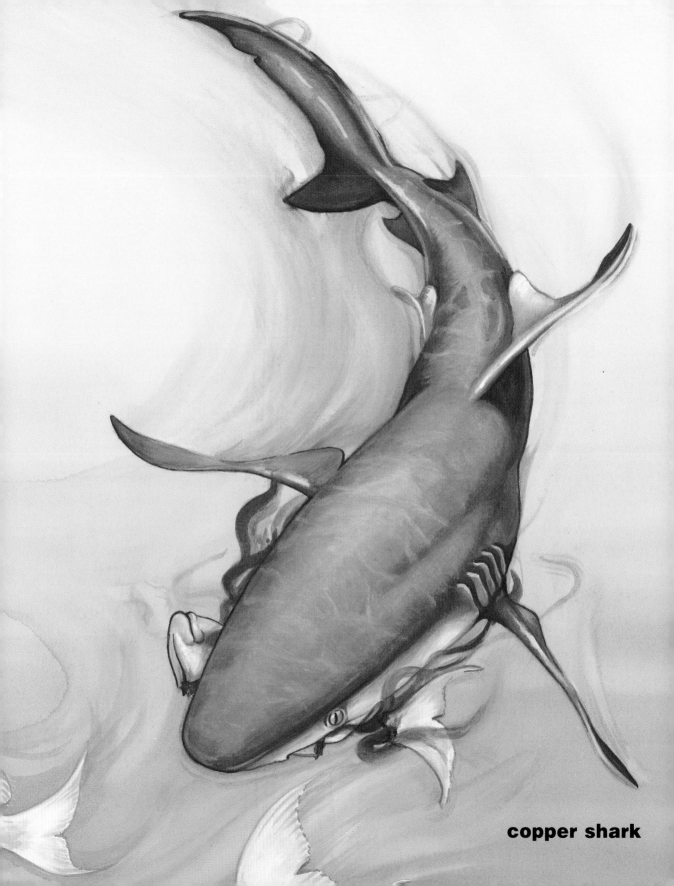

copper shark

A shark uses its teeth to kill its food. Its teeth are very big and very, very sharp. You have one row of teeth, but a shark can have 2, 3, 4, or even 5 rows of teeth at a time. When one set of teeth falls out, a new row grows in. An adult shark can grow a new row of teeth every 5 or 6 weeks. A baby shark grows a new row of teeth every 7 or 8 days!

A shark's jaws are very strong.

A shark can open wide and take a big, big bite!

grey nurse shark

Some sharks can go for days without eating. But when a shark finds food, it eats and eats and eats. Sharks may eat fish, whales, turtles, crabs, and other things that swim in the sea.

Sometimes sharks eat funny things, too. One shark ate two cans of peas. One shark ate a coat. Another shark ate a clock. Another shark ate a bag of rocks.

thresher sharks

Many people think sharks are "man-eaters." A few sharks, like the bull shark or the great white shark, are dangerous. They can bite people. But no shark goes hunting for people. Most sharks stay away from places where people swim.

Very few sharks have ever killed people, but many people hunt and kill sharks. In Japan, England, and other places, people like to eat shark meat.

Scientists like Dr. Eugenie Clark hunt sharks, too. They find sharks and study the things sharks do.

For a long time people did not think that sharks could sleep. But Dr. Clark saw undersea caves filled with sleeping sharks.

grey reef sharks

For a long time people did not think that sharks could learn. But Dr. Clark showed that sharks could learn. She trained some sharks in her lab to do tricks. The sharks could ring a bell to ask for food.

What other new things will scientists find out about sharks? Not even Dr. Clark knows that! But she and other scientists do know that it will be a long, long time before we find out all that there is to know about sharks.

lemon sharks

Sharing the Joy of Reading

Beginning readers enjoy reading books on their own. Reading a book is a worthwhile activity in and of itself for a young reader. However, a child's reading can be even more rewarding if it is shared. This sharing can enhance your child's appreciation — both of the book and of his or her own abilities.

   Now that your child has read **Sharks, Sharks, Sharks**, you can help extend your child's reading experience by encouraging him or her to:

- Retell the story or key concepts presented in this story in his or her own words. The retelling can be oral or written.

- Create a picture of a favorite character, event, or concept from this book.

- Express his or her own ideas and feelings about the subject of this book and other things he or she might want to know about this subject.

Here is a special activity that you and your child can do together to further extend the appreciation of this book: Sharks are a fascinating subject that your child might wish to know more about. You and your child can visit your local library to find other books about sharks. Read these books together. What information in the books does your child already know? What information about sharks is new? You can ask your child these questions as you read the books, or after you have finished them.